Warning

Poetically Unfiltered & Unfukked

V. S. Owen

Table of Contents

1. Accepting Responsibility 1

2. Learn To Control Your Environment............................. 3

3. Make A List 7

4. A List Explaining Why You Want These Things? 9

5. Monitor What You Allow into Your Mind 11

6. We Are as We Think... 13

7. Explaining the Subconscious Mind 15

8. Adopt a Positive Mental Attitude 17

9. Be Done with Anything of a Negative Vibe.................... 22

10. Identify Your Fu***Ps and Change What You Desire to Change.. 25

11. Stay Consistent: Routine Leads to Success.................... 28

12. Habits Are Learned and They Can Be Unlearned........ 29

13. Why Do You Want These Changes to Take Place? 30

14. Don't Expect Your Change To Come Easy 31

Dedications.. 34

An Empath's Worth 36

When Easy and Happy Are So Unfamiliar 37

Deep Thoughts 38

Things Never Said.. 39

Main Character 40

Sometimes... 41

I Felt It.. 42

Five Tools 43

I can See my Demons... 45

I See 46

A Symphony of Scars 47
Achieving Greatness 48
Burning Heart... 49
Proud of Me.. 50

I was born in September 1986 in North Philly to my Mom (Venessa Owen) and Dad (Michael Owen); they were married in April of 1980. My mom had lost 2 kids before she and my dad had me, and I am the older sibling between my brother and myself. From the time I tried to make my entrance into this world up until now, life has been throwing obstacles my way. My mom was in a bus accident when she was eight months pregnant with me; the doctors told her to prepare to bleed me out. My mom said, "hell no, I'm having my baby." She lay on the couch with her feet up, and she would lay where one would normally sit. She did this for about two to three weeks, if I remember correctly. The point is, she held me up there.

Once my mom and dad made it to the delivery room with the doctors two days after my due date, they encountered another problem. I had the umbilical cord wrapped around my neck. Even at that small age, I somehow got out of the umbilical cord, and I am alive. I flew out of my mom, though, because the doctor told her to push really well one more time. Well, when she did, I flew out of the doctor's arms and into my dad's arms. Daddy was saving me since day one.

As far back as history has been recorded, people have been getting fukked. Millions have been unnecessarily fukked over, under, and sideways. Fukked by family, fukked by friends, and especially fukked over by the government and the ruling class. If you happen to be African American, then you were pretty much born fukked; that's how it has always felt anyway. Maybe you were born to be a warrior out here and unfukk every situation that you felt has ever held you back. I want this book to tell a lot of my truth about how I've been fukked in my life and about how I learned to get unfukked. Nobody can unfukk you but you.

My mom passed away in March of 2009 when I was four months pregnant with my second child. After that happened, it seemed like I began to go through so much. It honestly felt like I was being fukked every way but right.

I gave birth to my son in October of 2009. DHS became involved because they found marijuana in his system. I was having bad contractions before I went in and decided to smoke a joint. I should have never done it, but I did. I recognized the part I played and accepted the fact I was the catalyst. Now, keep in mind I already had a child; she was three at the time, and I was doing pretty well as far as taking care of her. However, because my son was born with some weed in his system, I now had DHS breathing down my back. All I could think to myself was wow, I've been fukked. Technically speaking, I had been. However, I did it to myself. If I never smoked that weed, they would not be all up in my business. It took me years to take responsibility for that, but I finally did. I take responsibility for that and so many other things.

The Compound Effect worked against me instead of for me, but that was my own fault. It is imperative to stop blaming other people for what happens in our lives, especially when we're the catalyst. That's just the first step to becoming unfukked.

1. Accepting Responsibility

Accepting responsibility has got to be one of the hardest things a person has to learn to do. It's just easier to shift blame onto someone else. How convenient! My mother this; my father that; the WHITE MAN...

Accept that you have an issue/obstacle that needs resolving, whether internal or external, then take needed actions to overcome it. When a situation comes up and you feel ******, you must ask yourself this. What part did I play in this outcome? What could I have done differently to steer the situation in a different direction and a favorable outcome?

I remember the first time I was ever arrested. Yeah, you heard that right. I've been arrested before, twice actually. Anyway, the first time I called myself going to help a friend out. I helped my friend out, but I screwed myself over in the process. I definitely handled the little bully chick, but I also opened myself up to have a police record. I had never been arrested before, never even been in trouble or anything, and looking at the injuries to this girl. I was shitting bricks; OK, I was scared. I had a 3-month-old daughter at the time, and I was just trying to finish school at Lincoln Tech. The very next day after I had gotten arrested was my last day of school too. So, I was pissed the hell off, I almost missed signing the attendance sheet and all that, but I managed to make it.

All that, however, was all on me. I made the decision to go around to my girlfriend's house, and I also made the decision to handle her bully the way that I did. It was all me. I had to learn that, though, because at the time, if you asked me, shorty brought all that on herself. Bullies eventually get bullied, and that may be true, but I did not have to be the one who taught her the lesson. Nowadays, I leave it up to God.

2. Learn To Control Your Environment

I fukked myself right into that situation. In learning to accept responsibility for things, I've realized that certain people, places, and things could no longer be in my circle. It wasn't that I didn't love my people because I did and still do. I, however, love myself more, and I had to start controlling my environment.

My environment needed to be calm, cool, and covered by the grace of God if I'm keeping it all away 100. I had to let a friend go because she tried to tell me what I needed to take off of my social media one day. Not only that, but she was also upset with the way I chose to handle things for my mental health. I told her that we could just talk on the phone. We didn't have to be social media friends. I wasn't saying we couldn't be friends. However, I was dealing with a lot at the time, and I needed to protect my mental space. She was not trying to hear it, so she had to go. She cussed me out so badly on Facetime, and the whole time, I was just looking at her. Anybody who knows me, though, knows what I had to say: have a nice life, and when I say that, I really do mean it. If my friends or even my family cannot respect the things I want for myself, then they can have a nice life without me in it; it's as simple as that.

Once we become adults, we control who gets to stay in and out of our environment; that is the good thing about being grown. If we have people with negative energy in our circle, then they must vacate the peaceful community that we call our minds. If your mind is full of garbage, gossip, and other people's business, then that means you are not filling it with what it needs to be filled with, which is peace, love, and prosperity. Cliché, you say, well, how about this?

I had a friend; we're going to call him Jimmy. Jimmy was involved with this girl; we will call her Kate. They were involved for like 10 years. This girl did things just the way that she knew Jimmy wanted them done to portray herself as being something that she was not. Now me and Jimmy were close, so whatever he went through, I would know and vice versa. This girl attempted to beat Jimmy down without a pot to piss in or a window to throw it out. This baffled me, but not that much because my son's father did the exact same thing to me. Every time Kate tried to beat Jimmy down, he came back better and stronger than before. And once he realized that it was over for Kate. He eliminated her from his environment and has been taking off ever since. He made his mind a peaceful community, and his home was no longer filled with hatred and resentment. Once he was alone with no one but himself, he was finally able to blossom. He even began looking at life with a more positive aspect.

I met my son's dad when my mom was sick with cancer. I couldn't leave very far because I was the one who was at home taking care of her. Plus, I was the only one who could make anything the way her tastebuds desired. He lived across the street, and I could get him to run and grab little things for me since I couldn't go. We started to chill together, smoking, watching movies, and whatnot. Slowly, things changed; we became a couple, and now we have a son together. I love my son and don't regret him at all, I just wish I would have been done with his dad a lot sooner. This man put me through hell. He had trust issues that I had never even witnessed, and he's older than me by 14 years. I cried so many nights because he wanted the respect of a man, but he had no idea how to be one. He thought that because he was older than me, he knew more than I did. And sometimes that is true, but he has always needed me. Even after we broke up, whenever he needed somewhere to stay, he would always call me. He wasn't doing anything but dimming the light on my peaceful community. If I'm being honest, he is probably the biggest issue that I had as far as controlling my environment. I loved him, I still have love for him, but he had to go. I was with him for 11 years, and for the 5 that we broke up, he still stayed with me for 3-4 of those years because he couldn't do it on his own. All he was doing was stopping my shine. He had to go. Controlling my emotions with him around was hard as hell. So, how was I supposed to control my environment?

I had to change it; I had to change my environment and quickly. My mind was dark, cloudy, and even negative at times. The home was not a place I looked forward to going to. I dreaded when it was time to walk in the door. It was like when I was outside, I got more peace. I had to change that; it was making every day harder. Once I did change my environment by eliminating a certain person; I began to feel elevated. I didn't feel any more anger, hate, or anxiety; all that was over now. I finally had peace, along with a clear mind.

Doing the right thing is not always easy, and sometimes it can hurt so bad that you are unsure if you're doing the right thing at all. But once you do switch it up, meaning change your environment and the people that you allow into it, you'll feel that new feeling, that calm, easy feeling; then you'll know that you're moving in the right direction. Once you feel this feeling, you genuinely want to hold on to it. So, keep eliminating anybody who does you no good at all. Elevation is the Goal.

If a person doesn't benefit you, why are you letting them stick around? Please don't say oh, that's selfish because I don't even want to hear that. What it is is being mindful. People with nothing to lose don't care if they come along and fukk, your shit all up. If I'm being honest, that's exactly what they want to do. So, you see, it is imperative that you are selfish with your mind and the space you allow people to occupy in it.

3. Make A List

Make a list of what you want physically, what you want in your personal life, and what you want as far as finances.

In the physical aspect of my list I personally wanted to lose more weight and get in shape. So, every day, I started to walk. I made that a part of my daily routine, I began putting a workout routine on top of the daily walking routine that happened. That's what you want, it then becomes a habit, then a hypnotic rhythm. What is hypnotic rhythm? Hypnotic Rhythm is when a habit becomes a habit to which you devote no conscious attention. So, exercise became a part of my everyday life, which led it to become a hypnotic rhythm, which led to me losing weight and toning up.

Now, believe me, it sounds easy to do, but it is not easy at all. You literally have to begin to look at life like you're training in a marathon to live because you are. We are in a never-ending marathon because it doesn't end until we end. Meaning once we die that's when the marathon is over. That's it, and that is all.

When it came down to my personal life, all I wanted was peace. I figured one day, my mind wouldn't be so cloudy, and everything would begin to fall into place. I was in a very toxic relationship for 11 years; I do not regret it, though, because I learned so much, and I got my son out of it. I did learn that everyone doesn't love the way you may love, though, which will cause some confusion. I also learned that sometimes it is better to let things go. We called ourselves trying to make it work for the kids, but in the process, all we did was teach them toxic behavior. A lot of days, I did not want to come home because my environment was too toxic.

The time came, and I decided that enough was enough, and I wanted out of the relationship. This was not easy, but I knew I had one or two choices: end the relationship or lose my freedom. I love my freedom, so yeah, it was a wrap. After it was over and he was gone, I started reading more and just seeking to learn new information to sharpen my mind.

Once that began to happen, I felt like I finally got what I had been searching for for so long, and it never felt so good. So, my personal aspect of my list basically just shows you that I wanted peace; now, like I said, I want other things, but I had to find that first.

As far as my finances, I have my plan. Pay yourself out of each check. I say $50.00- $100.00 is good. It's a start, and that's what you have to do, get started. Now, I would like to help you develop one for your life.

4. A List Explaining Why You Want These Things?

I want to be around for a long time. I want to be able to guide my children into a future that they can be proud of. All that starts with the peace that you have or do not have. So, my why is easy: I want to be able to give my children knowledge as well as the opportunities that they deserve in this lifetime. Your list may be large, or it may be small, just keep it simple and continue to add to it whenever you feel the need. Also, remove things from the list as you begin to get them done. Actually, seeing your work on a list and removing 1 by 1 really helps. My reason for focusing on my children so much is easy... they are me. If they do great, then I have done great. Period!!!!

I went through a breakup while writing this book, and if I'm being honest, this breakup had me hurt in ways I thought I couldn't hurt anymore. I promised myself years ago, after my first love, that I would never feel like that again over a guy again, but I did. Actually, this one was worse, though, but only because he was my friend, my best friend. In the end, though, it came out that I was more of a friend to him than he ever was to me. That's how I felt anyway. I was really hurt because he talked about building businesses together and us getting married, and when he spoke about the future, he did include me. All of it was nothing but talk, though, and I expected that nonsense from other guys but not my best friend. That was traumatic for me. However, he was the one that I started my journey with on self-education. He put me onto a book, and it was up from there. So, if I'm being honest, when I think about him, it's bittersweet…. But at the same time, I'm grateful that we were able to learn so much together. He definitely hurt me, but from the hurt and pain that I felt, I channeled that energy into my writing and exercising. Those were the only things that helped me to feel better. I plan to use these tools everywhere in life because you cannot go wrong using them.

I've had friends contemplate suicide, and I would quickly explain to them why it was important to put those thoughts out of their minds. A lot of males and females contemplate suicide after a breakup, but that doesn't have to be the case, and every step that I talked about in the book is how that doesn't happen. Believe it or not, we all hold power within ourselves. We just have to learn how to use it. I'm telling you, when you do, you're going right past the sky and straight to the stars. You can't be stopped, and if you believe that, then you won't be stopped.

I've lost my mom and my dad, I've lost who I thought I was building a family with, and I've lost my home, but I managed not to lose my mind. The only way that was possible was me using these tools and keeping faith in my God. I look at this book as how my kids will get this knowledge (once they are old enough of course) and the tools they need to be successful. I wrote this in a language I think they and the generation they came up in will understand. I mean, let's be honest, people, as well as authors, have given great advice over the years, but their deliveries are sometimes boring and drawn out. I don't want mine to be like that, and I want to be heard loud and clear. So that's my reason and my why.

5. Monitor What You Allow into Your Mind

Just like we have to watch the food that we place into our bodies, we should also be doing that with our minds. I'm not much of a TV watcher never really have been. I also don't watch the news that much anymore. Why? That's easy: most of what comes on television is negative. So, if you are consistently watching negative things, then your mind is being fed negative impulses and vibrations. If you feed your mind horror, then you will always be scared. Feed it a bunch of reality TV; you will start to rate your life based on how they appear to be living theirs. If you are feeding your mind knowledge and inspiration, then that is what you will live, see, and experience every single day. I started to make it a priority to listen to an audiobook a day at least for 1/2 an hour. I began to train my mind to do that every single day, and it became a habit. After a while, I would be watching certain things, and if I felt any negative feelings about it, I just turned it off. If something did not sit well inside of my mind, it was a no-go for me; this was not just TV or social media either; I was like that with people too.

If you are always around someone who talks about people and gossips all the time, then that sinks into your subconscious. You want people who are uplifting others because that's love. We don't want to hang with people who tear people down. I want to network with people who genuinely want everyone to do good. I want everyone to do good, so naturally, those are the kind of people I want around me. As a man thinketh, then so is he.

This is why I don't allow certain people into my social circle. If it does not sit right in my spirit, I have no choice but to let you go. If you're into demons and all that weird stuff, keep it moving. If every word out of your mouth is vulgar and hurtful to someone in some way, then keep it moving. And believe me, I am always going to wish you the best, but that is going to have to be from a distance.

6. We Are as We Think

If you are out in these streets thinking that you are only good for what you have between your legs, then everything you get will be because of what you have between your legs. Now, I want you to really think about that for a minute because all that means is that you are selling yourself short. There are a lot of people out here that are willing to network and do business with you not based on what you have between your legs. However, if you just think that it is all about that, then it is always going to be all about that.

If you come up with something that you want to do but then you say to yourself," I'm tripping; I can't do this," then guess what? You won't do it. You have no idea what you are capable of until you make something up in your mind and stick to it. It all starts with a thought. I used to be one of them people who thought that was a load of BS. Honest to God, I was. But guess what? Not only do I believe it now, I live by it. If I have something I want to do, I put it in my mind, and I get it done, just like I did with my book. I decided on April 25th, 2021, that I was going to write this book. I started the book on April 27th, 2021. Today's date is May 3rd, 2021. Right now, while I'm writing this book, it's May 3rd, 2021, at 7:55 PM. I had an intention; I turned that into an action, and I then turned my action into a practice. The writing became consistent, which turned into a habit, and it slowly became a part of who I was becoming. My laptop will be here on Friday. I had a thought with the help of a friend, and the rest will forever be history.

You cannot sit around doubting yourself because when you do that, it is kind of like setting a booby trap against yourself, how you ask. Cool, let me explain. When you think negative thoughts, your subconscious mind automatically causes responses and actions to come from you with no thought of it. You will literally be reacting to things negatively just because, in your subconscious mind, you already have a negative outlook on the situation. So, who is setting who up? Right, you are setting yourself up. This right here is what people seem to have a hard time understanding. But the longer you take to understand it the longer it's going to take you to get unfukked.

7. Explaining the Subconscious Mind

Our subconscious mind is something that we rarely think about, and to communicate with your subconscious mind, you must first understand it. People make conscious decisions every day without a thought about what their subconscious mind is feeling. The mind stores feelings, urges, and memories that are far beyond our conscious minds. So, you can up and decide that you want to start doing something or stop doing something, but unless it's already inside of your subconscious, chances are, you will suffer temporary defeat.

However, consciously, you can think every day about what you want or what you do not want. Once you do that, begin to place it into your mind, and over time, the subconscious mind will obey you. The conscious mind places commands, and the subconscious obeys. Therefore, if you want to start a new habit you must consciously place it into your subconscious mind. I am telling you: it is the only way.

I have been saying that I was going to write a book for a long time now. This book was inevitable, it's been in my subconscious mind now for years. However, until now, I've never consciously done anything about it. But now, every day and every night, I am thinking about this book. I feel like it's something that the world needs from me, and I will follow through. I've learned so much from 2020 through 2024, and honestly, I feel like keeping all this newfound knowledge to myself would be extremely selfish. The only thing that I acquire to be selfish with is my time and energy; I'm more than ecstatic to drop this knowledge, though. I've always moved on love and that is how I always plan to move. That positive mental attitude is embedded into my subconscious mind and no one could ever change that.

8. Adopt a Positive Mental Attitude

This one right here is extremely important because you cannot change a damn thing if you do not change that attitude. Now, of course, it makes sense to make it a positive mental change. When you think positive thoughts there is nothing that can move you. Negative Mental attitude causes anger, which leads to altercations that can turn into violence and sometimes even death. But for most people, it just leads to a life that most people would rather not live. A life full of hatred, jealousy, confusion, and torture on one's self. All of this is because you chose to walk around with this negative mindset that is not hurting anyone but yourself.

I had this friend who we will call Trina. She was a good friend. We were friends since middle school for her and high school for me, we were about three years apart in age. Anyway, she had what people would call a hard life. Her dad was old enough to be her grandfather, and he died when she was 12. She had a lot of older siblings, but none of them really wanted the responsibility of raising her. At 3:00 AM one morning, Trina called me crying. She said that her nephew was there trying to touch her, and her older brother wasn't there. Man, I went to my mom and dad's room and woke my dad up. I told him what was going on, and we went and got her. I have never played about my friends, not even at a young age. Anyway, after her dad passed away, she just, you know, felt like nobody really cared. She tried to fill the void with boys, but we all know they only wanted one thing. By the time she was 26, she had three kids and major drug problems. We even had a falling out because the drugs altered her mind and her behavior. I did not know who my friend was anymore, and all she ever said or talked about was how everybody was out to get her and always talking negatively. She definitely had an idea, and her mind was already in her subconscious mind that everybody was against her and life was always going to be hard. She had a Negative outlook on everything. It did not matter how positive anybody tried to be because of life and the things she went through already, she was just a negative energy, and it took a toll on her. DHS took her children from her one day. That is what killed her; after all the drugs she did in her short-lived life, taking her babies was what did it. A lot of people thought that she had ODed on drugs, but that was not the case at all. She died because she had given up and had given in to that negative energy that she always fed. Her kids are doing great, though; they appear to be at peace, and I sincerely hope that they are. The one thing I do know, though, is that Trina is finally at peace. Finally!!!

I cannot remember one time I saw her practice having a positive mental attitude. I have never had my kids taken away from me, so that is a pain that I do not know, but I was taken away from my kids for a little while. I never gave up, though. I used to get on people's nerves because I could see the good in any bad situation. For example, she could have gotten help. The system would have helped her get into a drug program, they would have gotten her right, and they would have given her a house. I suppose she felt like she couldn't do it, though; I guess that's why she gave up and died from a broken heart.

When we entertain these negative thoughts, we bring in sickness, poverty, depression, and even fear. I cannot stress how much I need you guys and girls to maintain a positive mental attitude. It will literally make or break you, kill or save you. It killed my friend, don't let it kill any of you. When you hear those evil whispers, quickly replace them with 3 positive thoughts.

A friend is someone who makes you feel good about yourself; I do not need judgmental friendships. As a friend, I will tell you what you need to hear, and that is it. I will not drill my friends about their wrongdoings; I am not a yawl mom; it's up to you to make necessary changes for your life. I really do expect the same from my friends.

I hate when someone tries to dictate my life to me. My life is mine, so let me have it. Now, I am a Virgo, so that simply means if you are unhappy with Venesha, then you can leave the baby. Lol, ain't nobody stopping you. I despise the back and forth especially when it's for years. If you have a problem with little ole me, then leave me where the hell I am at because I guarantee that's where I would leave you. I used to look at it like I wasted time with certain friends, but not anymore, though. It all had to happen so that I could distinguish what was and was not acceptable behavior from people.

Since I was last writing, I found out that my dad has stage 3 Cancer. It was 12/02/2022 when I found out about the Cancer and 12/12/2022 when we found out where it was. He was diagnosed with Liver and esophagus cancer. I believe I was coming home from my son's school when he called and told me. After we hung up, I stopped right there on like 16 &

Oregon Ave and just started balling. I waited until we hung up to break down because, I mean, shyt, he was going through enough. He was the one who had Cancer, so I didn't want to make him feel worse for making me cry. Even at 36 years old, I am still and will always be my daddy's little girl. My brother not being around at the time didn't help either. I was so scared; I lost my mom already, and I was really not ready to lose my dad. But are we ever ready to lose the ones we love? The answer is no, but that does not change the fact that we're still going to lose them. Whether to death or life itself, we lose people every day. You have to learn to be ok with that because you can't control It. I think losing my mom taught me that, and that friend that I lost to. I lost my mom to death, and I lost her to life first, then death.

While writing this book, my dad passed away. He passed away on December 3, 2023. Needless to say, maintaining a positive mental attitude was not easy. It did hurt when I lost my mom, but since my dad was still here, it helped. When Big Mike passed away, I felt alone. My safety net was pulled right from under me. It honestly may have been the hardest death I think that I ever had to deal with. Now, keep in mind that I didn't live with my dad; I have my own place. I just always felt safe with him here. My vision was cloudy for maybe the first week after his death, and his funeral was on December 21, while my dead mom's birthday was the very next day. SMH, talking about grief. I could feel depression trying to ease its way back into my life, but maintaining a Positive Mental Attitude allowed me to stop that from happening.

I was extra sad because my brother had been wrongfully held in prison for almost 4 years and was literally marked free to go on December 6, 2023. Three days after my Daddy passed away, my brother was set free. My cousin said that my dad went up to heaven, choking the angels and telling them to free his son. Lol, that was the way it seemed, and it added some humor to a painful time.

Lucky for me, that friend that I had tried dating and it didn't work; he had my back. Over time, we learned how to talk to one another instead of talking to one another. I thank the man upstairs that I learned about maintaining a PMA because my friend said that I handled my dad's death very well, and I'm sure it was because I had his support. Don't get me wrong, my Daddy was getting me ready for it for years, but it's nothing like having a friend when it happens. I had to get out of my head, allowing my emotions to get in the way. I needed someone around who knew me. Now granted, he didn't know everything I was going through, and he still doesn't, but he knew what words to say to me and what books to throw my way whenever I appeared to be on a downfall. He knew how to get me back to my positive mental attitude, and when you're grieving, that's exactly what you need.

9. Be Done with Anything of a Negative Vibe

This may be the most important section in this book. I say that because it doesn't matter how much work you do on yourself. If you are in constant contact with negative energy, you will turn negative. Negative energy spreads like wildfire or like rotten apples. The only way to get rid of it is to be done with it all together. I've had to leave friends alone because of their negativity. If every time you say something, your friend is like yeah, but this and that could be a problem, then they are the problem.

My best friend just recently called me while I was at work, right? God's honest truth. She had a dream about me and one of my friends I actually stopped dealing with while finishing this book. Anyway, she basically had a dream that Shorty was trying to get me killed. This was weird for her to have this dream, but she did, and she called me to let me know. Now, the friend that she was referring to came to find out practiced which spells. To each, they own, but that explained so much about her. I used to think maybe God didn't want me to be her friend because she had a thing with flies. Or flies had a thing with her; all I knew was wherever she was, they wanted to be. She was negative, and I loved her, but she ain't love me, so Fukk Her.

Then there was the druggy. I'm literally shaking my head while writing this. I pray she gets it together. But she was negative too. I would see her calling and look up to the heavens because all she did was complain. I honestly don't know how we were even friends for so long. But once the drugs played a factor, it was a wrap. She became this person I did not know. She definitely hid her actual self from me. It was like she didn't want me to know her actual thoughts. I was like yeah, I'm signing the fukk off. I don't have time to keep looking over my back at these so-called friends.

When it came to my baby's father, his negativity was too much for me because he lived with me. He looked at himself as a critic but came off as a hater to me. By all means, say whatever it is that you want to say, and then shut the fukk up. PLEASE. He never knew when to shut up, and living with that was just too much for me. I will always have love for that man, but we cannot effectively live together under the same roof. Ima always wants him to be great moving forward, but I must watch over my own mental first.

So, from this moment forward, if anyone gives me a red flag, PEACE!!!!!! And I say it with love. But the negativity has no place in my mind or atmosphere. I said all that to ya'll to say this. I stopped being friends with all of these people in (2021), and God is working on me. You're not going to get any of your blessings if you try to keep negative vibes around your positive vibes. The two do not go together; they are just like oil and water, and it is never going to mix. No matter how much you try, the two will never go together. That's why this is the most important part of this book because you can do everything I tell you to do. If you don't eliminate the negative energies, then you're not really doing anything. I mean, you may learn new things, but it'll never get you nowhere because, like I said 3 times before, maybe even more, the two do not mix.

For reasons only God knows the answers to, I had to leave these people alone. I may think I know why, I might even be right, but I leave all of that up to God. I throw up my hands. I let it all go because regardless of what any of them may have thought, they were all expendable. I only have room for positivity going forward. When my bestie called me about that dream, she was frantic. She legit wanted me to watch out for Shorty, and I felt nothing but love from her, like I always do. So, of course, Ima keeps her; that's my baby.

10. Identify Your Fu***Ps and Change What You Desire to Change

I have this friend, more like a sister, and she's been being used by the people closest to her. She's really good at the credit game, and people know that, and because people know that, they always expect a lending hand from her. It's not that she has a problem saying no either, but sometimes she just wanted to avoid the drama. She owned her first house for about 15 years, and the day she moved into her second house, all types of shyt seemed to have happened. Every year spent in her home, she had felt trapped in a way because her boyfriend was on the lease with her, and every time they would argue or get into a disagreement, there was nothing that she could do because he was on the lease. Before she moved into her new home the bank teller asked her if her boyfriend would be going onto the lease with her. She said yes to the bank teller, telling her to add his name to the documents. Immediately after doing that, they got into an argument; she said sis, "I called that lady back no less than 10 minutes later, telling her to take his name off."

The people behind the money were initially the problem; however, because of what I would always say to myself, my subconscious mind picked that up and ran with it. Now I was out here missing my blessings.

Once I had identified that thoughts and statements were fukkin me up, I stopped. I began saying nothing but positive things until I made myself believe it. If I did not believe it yet,

I would say it until I did. Nothing will change if your subconscious is not buying whatever you are selling.

Of Course, there was more to my list, but after educating myself about myself, that's what I knew I really wanted to focus on. Like I said earlier, my own thoughts and statements were setting myself up for failure. I know, right? I could not freaking believe it. However, once I changed it all up, things have been working out in my favor even more.

Throughout my whole journey, I learned that I had to Unfukk myself. I had to alter my moods, and I had to change my attitude. Bad things are going to continue to happen; you must learn to control your emotions and reactions. That's the key. You can't take everything so personally; you'll give yourself stress levels that were never necessary. I lost my daddy while I was writing this book and slowly gained so much peace. Both of my best friends were such a tremendous help. One of them was an immense help in a very weird way.

I gave up cigarettes while finishing this book and I feel so good because of it. Me and the bestie made a bet that if I smoked a cigarette, I would have to put on a Cowboy's jersey and take a damn picture in it. We just knew that was not happening. He's a cowboys fan, and I am a diehard bleed green Eagles fan. The bet was made on February the 2nd, 2025. This was literally a week before Super Bowl 59. He would have to put on an Eagles jersey and take a pic or give me 300.00. All I knew was I was not putting on a damn Cowboy Jersey. I felt like my Daddy might just rise from the dead angry if I put on some Cowboys Jersey. That was all I knew, and it was all I needed to know. My Birds bussed Kansas City Ass on the 9th. So you know I was not picking up any cigarettes at all. I still can't believe it was a bet that had me stop smoking. I still have not picked one up at all. Who would have thought that a team that I despise was the reason I gave up Cigarettes? Honestly, I'd like to thank the Cowboys Foundation.

I realized that in giving up cigarettes, I was unknowingly gaining something back that I had lost a while ago. I regained self-respect and dignity. I would allow people to say certain things to me, and I'd just brush it off because I didn't want any altercations. However, when you develop this habit, people are more likely to come at you with the bullshyt because they know that they can rely on you, not saying anything at all. So yeah, it was time for a change.

I'm already aware of the issue I have around my cycle with the PMDD, so I'm already aware of things I need to work on. I will not roll with people who can only see my faults because none of us are perfect, and we all have faults of our own.

Life really is a never-ending journey because now I'm going into the part of life where I sweat at night. I don't think I have ever prayed so much in my life as much as I do now. One thing I learned is that all of this is mental. Lifer is a mental exercise. Mind over matter, and that will help with so much, from symptoms, sickness, and even addictions. It's all mind over matter.

I am so sure that a lot of people think that I am crazy and trust me, that is fine. However, I learned to protect my environment, and I learned to let things go. Iver developed this feeling of peace that I cannot explain. I can tell you that I love it, though, and I can tell you that I want you to feel this feeling of peace too.

11. Stay Consistent: Routine Leads to Success

Once you write out your list and begin to change things, make sure that you stick with it and stay consistent. To kill one habit, you must become consistent with another positive one.

When I started exercising, I had some days where I was not consistent. But I always had more consistent days than non-consistent days. Even if I was not exercising, I was thinking or contemplating exercising, which, in most cases, led me to exercise. Staying consistent and following a routine is not easy at all, but it is very necessary. See, routine leads to discipline, and when you have discipline, you also have control. What better to have control over than yourself? If you have control over yourself, then you have it all under control; it really is as simple as that.

I told y'all how I had been locked up and even did some probation time. I had to stay consistent in staying out of the bullshyt. It was hard not to smack some bitches, believe me. But I had to switch it up or else the routine that I had been so used to was going to keep me in a lot of trouble. I'm talking 5 years in Munsee trouble. At the end of the day, it was trouble that I did not want. So, I began to let shyt slide. If a bitch was talking shyt that is exactly what it was as far as I was concerned, shyt I did not care about. I even stopped going out so much because I did not want to have to smack somebody just because they were drunk and out of line. To avoid all of that I just eliminated myself from certain scenes that were once a part of my routines. I told you, though, that my routines were leading to nothing but failure. So, I had to switch it up and stay consistent.

12. Habits Are Learned and They Can Be Unlearned

Anything that you learn, you can unlearn. Do not ever think that just because you grew up learning things a certain way, that's the only way. You can always learn something new. People switch religions all the time because they learn something new. People switch political parties because they learned something new. You can always unlearn negative behavior if you replace it with positive behavior. However, if you keep making excuses as to why you can't change, then you will not change. Why? Because your subconscious mind knows how you really feel, which is inadequate to what you desire.

You do not want to cancel out the good you're trying to do with destructive thoughts which leads to destructive behavior. (As long as your desires are bigger than your failures, then you will be exquisite.)

13. Why Do You Want These Changes to Take Place?

Why do you want anything to change in your life at all? Why do you feel fukked? And what is your reasoning for wanting to become unfukked? Most people just think about what it is that they want, but they never take the time to consider why they want it in the first place. Why is it important, though very important? When you know why, then so does your subconscious mind. Now, we all know that once your subconscious becomes aware of anything, it will cause you to consciously do things to move your life in the direction you desire.

If every day you wake up thinking that you want this dream car, subconsciously, you will begin doing things that will lead you to get the car. You're going to work harder; you may even take on jobs that you usually would never consider. But because you want this car so bad, you do things out of the ordinary. That all has to do with the subconscious mind I have been talking to you about. Your subconscious mind is thinking about why you want these changes, and your conscious mind goes out to get them.

14. Don't Expect Your Change To Come Easy

When COVID-19 hit the U.S., I was sick (mentally), scared, and terrified. I felt helpless and weak because there was nothing I could do to make the outside safe for my babies and myself. Personally, I was out of work for 13 months, all because of my fear of Covid and bringing it home to my babies. My therapist was worried that I was going to get violent with people. She was probably right too, because as far as I knew, if you got too close to me, coughing or sneezing, it was a major problem; the unknown is scary. I stayed in the house for 13 months, and I honestly feel like I showed a lack of faith in my God. However, I have all the faith in my God. We eventually did catch it in 2022. I caught it three times, but God was merciful to me and my babies. This pandemic has taught me to do exactly what I was telling y'all to do. When a negative thought attempted to enter my mind, I would say, "I'm not catching no damn Covid, and neither are my kids." People thought I was crazy for saying and believing that. However, when we did catch it, it was sweet. We really just felt like we had a cold, no temperatures or anything, and we're all asthmatics. So, you see, even when we are sick, we are good, and we are going to remain healthy, PERIOD!!!! I decided to Adopt a positive mental attitude and just roll with that. It wasn't easy, but it was very much necessary. It was necessary because the fear I was feeling was holding me back from living basically. I wouldn't work, and going out to have a good time was a hell no for me. Covid was controlling my life. Now, of course, I'm going to do what must be done to stay safe, but I was just stuck in the house. I felt like I was trapped in a prison, or maybe it was just the prison in my mind. The point is I felt stuck, and my anxiety, sheeesh that went through the roof.

I've been prolonging finishing and releasing this book for a while now. My dad really wanted me to get it out there, and we all know that I'm a daddy's girl. So, Ima just get it done. He always told me that I am a writer and that now is the time to become an author. He was right, so I'm going to stop procrastinating and just print this thing. Honestly, I felt like my book was too short, but if I can say everything that needs to be said in a shorter period of time, then I am sure that a lot of you would appreciate that.

Since I was last working on my book, a lot has changed. Some things have changed for the last time, and some things have started fresh. For me my thirties have been a constant learning experience about everything. I read this year on Instagram that our thirties are nothing but research; it's not until our forties that we actually start living. I genuinely felt that because, in my thirties, I think that I learned the most. When I say everything, I mean everything; friendships, relationships and situationships. I have been involved in every one of them, and the easiest way to get out of it is to stay out of your own head.

I'm pretty much at peace now, but we all know that the devil stays busy. He'll creep into your mind like a thief in the night, where we are all human. You have to exercise your mind and strengthen your mental muscles; you'll be fine.

Trying to control someone else's actions other than your children is a form of toxicity. You will hear a person say, "But I just want better for you," and sometimes it's genuine, but still, they are just trying to justify their bullshit. Your life is your life, and you move on your time and at your own damn pace. If your pace is too slow for someone then tell them it's been great, but it's time we move in separate directions.

I lost another friend in 2022 to this pill epidemic. She is still alive, but you know, just barely. I am saying all of this to say that, as you can see, you will lose, but most of the time, what you were holding on to was only holding you back.

So let it go, let it all go. You have to Unfukk yourself. People are always going to be out there to play the devil; just learn to deal with that; that's life. But remember that you have the power to make the choices needed to pick yourself up out of anything.

Dedications

I'd like to take this time to dedicate this book to My Dad. I promised him that I would get it done, so that is what I had to do. He and my mom raised me to be a strong woman. My mom used to tell him that he was a little too raw with me, and maybe he was cause I'm as raw as they come. Sometimes, being too raw will only hurt you, though, and it doesn't matter if you are a man or a woman. You have to know when to relax and let things go. Of course, my dad tried on numerous occasions to explain this to me, but I had to go through experiences first. I had to learn on my own. Now I feel like I finally have the balance that he was so proud of when he passed on.

I would also like to thank my friends: the ones who I still call my friends and the ones who have moved on. If it wasn't for you guys and the experiences that we shared then I never would have learned what I needed to learn about Life. Education is great, but experience is greater. Without those experiences, I would never have been able to identify an energy vampire. You can read up on these things and get all of the education in the world, but if you don't go through experiences to experience it, then it's all useless, and you can't really explain anything to anyone else since you don't really know. Once again, I thank every one of you. I am in a much more peaceful place.

Of course, I thank my kids for always asking me if I finished the book yet. They always kept it on my mind. They would never let me forget about it. I love my babies.

Last but not least, I thank my brother. When my Daddy died, that was hard, and I felt like nobody was there because he was still locked up. I thank him for getting out when he did and just for being the best brother a girl could ask for.

I decided to give my readers some of my poetry because that's a lot of what came out of me during my times of grief, pain, and misunderstanding and healing.

An Empath's Worth

I am a person that can feel another person's joy, my skin bumps up, and the tears, they deploy.

I can feel exactly what it is that your feeling, this also includes the sadness and healing.

The madness, the drilling, all the inner feelings. All lined up so delicately on glass ceilings.

I get to feel all your anger and rage, I feel when you say fukk it and turn the page.

I feel it in my gut when you feel like a puppet, I feel when the tides are high and you bluffing.

I feel when your nights are lonely and your feeling cold, I feel when you're riding high and feeling bold.

The point that I'm making, is that I feel it all. Sucks all my energy out like air from a ball.

I sit here and I pray, taking energy back from the earth, because when I make people feel good it's a rebirth.

It's an earth orgasm and most people can't fathom, I have natural energy like light from a candle.

Like pain from a hammer going straight in your back, but my energy is positive, so it won't feel like that.

It'll feel more like a cold beer after work, or maybe even a good game after church.

Something like meds after getting hurt, or even the joy one feels after childbirth.

And this is the volume of an Empath's worth.

When Easy and Happy Are So Unfamiliar

When easy and happy are so unfamiliar,
When you actually feel it, it's a little peculiar.
A little bewildered is what you begin to experience.
It's not making any sense, so you're not tryna hear of it.
The yin in you is on go and ready to feel,
Yang yelling, "Hell no!" it's too scared, for real.
Too scared to go forward and be pushed ten steps back,
Too scared to feel good, 'cause life don't life like that.
Life don't cut a price like that; I mean, that's our way
of thinking,
And that is the problem. That's our way of sinking.
Please understand what I'm saying: you gotta take that
step,
You gotta make that move. You gotta prep that prep.
Listen to me. Easy and happy are not that unfamiliar,
And you have to stop looking at it as being peculiar.
I don't know about y'all, but I'm ready for my presents,
Been through enough bullshyt, and more than enough
lessons.
More than enough stressings from more than enough
peasants,
And now I'm welcoming all things good to me.
I'm taking all of God's blessings.

Deep Thoughts

Have you ever tried to get so deep inside your own head your mind bled

Have you ever tried to see so clear but all you could see was blood smeared

Your head is throbbing, your eyes are sobbing

It's so much commotion inside ya own head with yourself you stay mobbing

Can you understand what I'm saying, you in a fight with yourself

Can't nobody else help you, your in a fight for your health

Your in a fight for clarity, in a tug of war with confusion

And you can't tell real from fake because your mind is an illusion

Your mind stays tripping, you never trying to outlive

You eat with your eyes to much on your plate and miss what the world actually has to give

Meanwhile you're out here hating to live, hating what God gives

Forgetting in your heart is exactly where God lives

Things Never Said

A dream is nothing but something you wake up from, and life is just something we succumb to. Obstacles will pass, while some troubles will last. Sometimes, the temp can be 190 in the kitchen, and life can feel like a never-ending mission. No opposition, steadfast, and hold your position. My words hit curbs, then they slightly swerve, sometimes bussing a uey on quey they can be cold like icebergs. Or they can be warm like the water that boils, seeping into your soul like moisture into soils.

There comes the point where you're done with the turmoil; you're done with the resistance, and you're finished with the gargoyles. The gargoyles are a representation of people, and most of these people are dishonest and deceitful. Which is why I feel rage when I let the pen flow on this page. But when I hit the stage feels like I've been hit with sage. Hit with relief and an ease of the pain, I feel orgasms when I recite my pain. I am enlightened by this rain and my sense of humor; I do my best to maintain. It's hard to smile when you're the golden child, and at the same time, you're the one that's oh so wild.

You seem to be the one that's always on the run and you were always the one who was never trying to come: Home or to church, never trying to make it work, day by day, you just kept making it worse. Pay by pay, the wall is where you lay; you slay by day but in the pit is where you stay. You put on a good face when you hide behind them substances. It's time to break free, clear ya head, 'cause it's disrupting us.

Main Character

In this life I have the purest intentions, one is yin one is yang, they fall from different dimensions.

I've been loved indirectly, come to find out it was directly, he was always the one who really respected me.

Sometimes neglecting me, pushing me into action, occasionally pissing me off taking away from the satisfaction.

But as time moves on you realize that action is key, because action pushes you into practice and that's where you really get to see.

That you should keep practicing consistently, everything that he pushed my way it uplifted me.

Slowly but surely this consistent change became habit. And that habit became me because I just had to have it.

I just had to grab it cause this love is unconditional, nothing about this energy or love is traditional.

So, I just embrace it, whenever we get to be in bliss, I love his warm touch and i love to kiss those lips.

It makes all the fights had worth every lesson, and things were definitely sometimes stressing me.

But I know you are my blessing, and you are also the one I had to chill from neglecting, you are the one I love and who I grow with directly.

I stopped letting all the little BS upset me. I'm in love with your loyalty and the way that you direct me.

Sometimes

I sit here thinking faithfully, so that way everything
that I do, I do it gracefully.

Trying to get myself to perfect is a waste to me, and
sometimes it's nothing but a smack in the face to me.

Sometimes, it's just slowing up the race for me;
sometimes, it gets really hard to date for me.

Sometimes, it paces with me; sometimes, it waits for
me. And sometimes it'll get all up in ya face for me.

Sometimes, I need to pause for some time, Sometimes I
need a hidden clause on the lines.

Sometimes it's yours; sometimes it's mine. We need to
release energy to shine.

Sometimes we out, and sometimes we in. Sometimes
we must lose to win.

Some bring the light, some bring the grim, some will
secretly bite ya back out and try to run it again.

Sometimes you here with it, sometimes you there with
it and sometimes you don't know cause you ain't really
clear with it.

Sometimes we right, sometimes we wrong, and
sometimes just have to let God use us as his pawn.

I Felt It

I was sitting here watching this show, and I got hit with this crazy wave of emotions.

You ain't gonna understand that shyt hit my heart the way them whales dive into them oceans.

Tears rolling down my eyes, and I started calling on God, head feeling like it's in a dimension ride.

So Ima take that as grief and pain, that shyt can hit hot like acid rain.

I wasn't sitting here worried about one thing, I wasn't even waiting on my phone to ring, but I felt it.

And I don't know if I felt good or bad, not even sure if I was happy or sad.

Pops been gone a year me and the twin flame just split, after a quarter plus years it's time to change some shyt.

And I felt it, I made some changes in my life, I am hearing more from God, and I'm quite sure he just took me on my first spiritual ride, Cause I felt it.

Five Tools

We are living in a world where reversal desire is key.
You must trick your own mind to get to where you
really wanna be.
Reverse your desires, start embracing your pain,
Embrace everything that normally drives you insane.
Feel it, like it, allow it to flow through your veins,
And don't let none of the pain you're receiving be
taken in vain.
We must continuously dish out active love,
Because when confusion arises, the tongue tends to
judge.
Then the anger seems to budge a little into the wrong
direction.
Everything starts falling apart like an internal
dissection.
And then you hear a voice—that's your inner authority.
You hear what's being said, thanks to inner maturity.
You get a clearer picture of what you're supposed to
know,
And you'll finally learn to let things go,
And gracefully dip into that graceful flow.
In that grateful flow, you will find nothing but
greatness.
Nothing but peace, nothing but ease.
And that peace is something that you really wanna
have,

Because then that jeopardy won't seem so bad.
Jeopardy is something that we all fall into,
We just humans on earth; it's what we here to do.

I can See my Demons

I can see my demons, and baby, I can see them clear.

Some of your demons can be someone you hold dear.

And when being calm, cool, and collected won't get you respected.

That's when you're known to lash out, and people start feeling neglected.

Oh, you can hear me now, because I'm not being ladylike and discreet.

I'm not kissing your ass, and I'm not kissing your feet.

I'm known to say what needs to be said,

And I'm known to put some deep shyt in your head.

Some of these people will feel like an old cigarette.

They're just a terrible habit that you'll live to regret.

Your attitude gets so terrible when you're trying to dissect

Some shyt you clearly just need to leave alone and forget.

I See

When I look into your eyes, I see great things.

I see great value; I see deep pain.

I see fear, I see weird,

I see humbled, I see sneered.

I see a human being, who is only being human.

I see a weakened soul constantly being tormented.

I see anger, I see joy, I see a girl I see a boy.

I see in, I see out, I see fight without a doubt. I see day, I see night,

I see wrong, I see right, I see multiple personalities lingering in the night.

I can see the breakthrough as good as I can see the breakdown.

And when you finally let loose I see that soul taking its crown.

A Symphony of Scars

I heard a poem today, she talked about everything that I feel. Had me thinking how fast time moves, yet how long it takes to heal. I had to admit to myself that toxic traits are real. Depression a mfer and Anxiety a bully in the field. I'm not even ready to disclose my PTSD, but whether I'm ready or not, it's always ready for me. Whether I'm with it or not, it's always trying to be the center of attention that I'm never trying to see. I rarely try to mention negative vibes that I'm feeling, I think if I just ignore it, I can keep on concealing. I hate to feel complacent, like I'm pinned to a brick wall, no air pumping in my chest, I'm just ready to fall. I won't spend too much time here because I get sad, so I digress. I say a prayer, smoke a blunt and let the smoke flow in my chest, put them airpods in and them apple tunes be the best.

That's when I can feel the positivity flowing in my veins. That's when I finally feel like I'm sane. But just momentarily, it only acts as a band-aid. Cause its so many unreal people out here, it's like a fan page. It's like, the love is man-made, never coming from the heart; just like on them fan pages, they will tear you apart.

Achieving Greatness

As I achieve my greatness, it's a little bit scary as I'm slowly approaching success. I'm preparing my flowers to put on my bed for when they finally lay me to rest. I'm one step closer to this path that I've chosen, the one that leads me to glory. Believe you me I've been through some things so I'ma always have a story. It's like the greatness is finally approaching, I'm so excited that it's here. Proud to be moving forward but the human in me has some fear. My human nature gets a little sneered, a little happy mixed with sad. My darkened thoughts get a little risky, a little this and a little that. I do my best to remember, we are only here part of the time. And if you look real close, we are nothing but parts in time. A time comes when you feel your feet coming mysteriously off the ground, you'll slowly focus in noticing, it's all you's around.

Burning Heart

How can I find my soulmate steady rocking it out with my twin flame. We teaching each other lessons watching our love go down the drain. We signed up for this, before we ever even evolved. We agreed to this with no idea of the hidden clause. Pause, we got decades in together, and no matter how hard we try, we can't weather the weather. It's like no matter how hard we cry, we can't get it together, no matter how hard we study only for a minute is it better. This love is confusing, because when it's good it's great and twice as amusing. But when it's bad, we talking borderline hate with twice as much confusion. It's all an illusion that we create in our minds, and because of the connection, I felt I just knew you were my prime, it's like you were my rhyme. But I had to slowly come to see, I was doing as much to you as you were doing to me. So like you said, fall back, it's time to let things be. Time to have faith, unravel some things and see what we can see. I feel guilty for falling out of love with you, but I know that your love is falling for me to, I can feel it boo. I see it in your eyes when you looking at me and I can feel it with a kiss. Our souls are locked in as one, and the feelings we can try to dismiss. But we can't, it ain't no getting around this. We gotta go through this to meet our soulmates, we gotta teach each other how to clear our souls of hate, and that right there is how we'll be great.

Proud of Me

I know you been watching Mom, and I know you proud Dad. Yall sitting in heaven thinking damn we miss em bad. Y'all was here to see me wine, here to see me grind. But when it all went down y'all wasn't here to see the shine. Big bro miss you, the grandkids miss you, all we really wanted was to get to hug and trick you. Laugh a lil bit get some more time with you. But that was too much to ask, my man needed y'all fast, it was on some nut shyt now y'all a blast from the past, and it was on some tough shyt that cancer kicked y'all ass. Hated to see y'all go; but I hated seeing the pain. After y'all left it was rain on my brain, and when y'all checked, my only thoughts was changing the game. Mind got trippy thought about rearranging some lames, but it's all. Good now I won't name no names, You'll get no satisfaction cause I won't claim them lames.